**This book was
presented to
Mount Tamalpais
School Library
in honor of the
birthday of**

*Ryan McCauley*

this *11* day of *May* 19*93*

SIERRA CLUB
WILDLIFE
LIBRARY

# EAGLES

SIERRA CLUB
WILDLIFE
LIBRARY

# EAGLES

Text by Aubrey Lang

Photographs by Wayne Lynch

General Editor, R. D. Lawrence

Sierra Club Books | Little, Brown and Company
San Francisco | Boston • Toronto • London

First Edition

All photographs © Wayne Lynch, except the following: © G.R.
Bortolotti, 49, 51; © Peter Davey, 5, 12; © Pat J. Frere, 38; © Neil Rettig,
24, 62; © Robert R. Taylor, 13, 31

**Library of Congress Cataloging-in-Publication Data**

Lang, Aubrey.
Eagles / text, Aubrey Lang: photography, Wayne Lynch. – 1st ed.
    p.   cm. – (Sierra Club wildlife library)
Includes index.
    Summary: Introduces the physical characteristics, habits, and
habitats of the many eagle species.
    ISBN 0-316-51387-3
    1. Eagles – Juvenile literature.   [1. Eagles.]   I. Lynch, Wayne.
ill.   II. Title.   III. Series.
QL696.F32L34   1990
598.9'16 – dc20                                                                    90-8729

Sierra Club Books/Little, Brown children's books are published by
Little, Brown and Company (Inc.) in association with Sierra Club Books.

10 9 8 7 6 5 4 3 2 1

Published simultaneously in Canada by
Key Porter Books Limited

Printed in Singapore

# Contents

# The King of Birds

For centuries and throughout the world, the eagle has been a symbol of strength, courage, and power. In ancient Assyria the eagle was revered as a god. Persian armies and Roman legions carried banners with the image of the eagle on them into battle. Some native North American tribes, such as the Plains Cree, believed that the eagle had special powers and that these powers would come to anyone who owned parts of the bird. So tribe members collected eagle feathers, feet, and claws. The feathers were especially valued and were used on headdresses worn in important ceremonies. When a chief gave an eagle feather to a brave young warrior, this was considered a high honor. The totem poles of the Haida tribe in British Columbia have great eagles carved at the tops.

Many countries and groups have used the eagle as their emblem. It is found on buildings, monuments, and flags. The United States chose the bald eagle as its national bird. The highest rank in the Boy Scouts of America is the eagle scout. A terrific golf score is called an "eagle." And when U.S. astronaut Neil Armstrong landed the first manned vehicle on the moon, he said, "The *Eagle* has landed."

*The bald eagle is the national bird of the United States.*

GOLDEN EAGLE
(BOOTED EAGLE)

BALD EAGLE
(FISH EAGLE)

# Eagles of the World

There are fifty-nine *species*, or kinds, of eagles in the world, and they are found on every continent except ice-covered Antarctica. Some live in dense forests and tropical jungles; others live in high mountains or along the shores of lakes, rivers, and oceans; and still others live where there are no trees.

All the species can be divided into four major groups: fish eagles, snake eagles, giant forest eagles, and booted eagles.

BATELEUR EAGLE
(SNAKE EAGLE)

HARPY EAGLE
(GIANT FOREST EAGLE)

Bald Eagle

Bateleur Eagle

Harpy Eagle

Golden Eagle

WORLD DISTRIBUTION OF FOUR
SPECIES OF EAGLES

There are eleven species of *fish eagles*, and all of them are quite large. The most famous one is the bald eagle, the only fish eagle found in North America. The others live in Europe, Asia, and Africa, and some live on remote islands. Fish eagles usually live near oceans or lakes or rivers because, as you can guess, their favorite food is fish. These eagles have toes with rough bumps on them to enable them to hold on to their slippery prey.

*A pair of African fish eagles survey their territory.*

True to their name, *snake eagles* specialize in catching snakes. There are twelve kinds of them in the world, but none lives in North America. Most of these eagles live in Europe and Africa, and a few live in Asia, India, and the Philippines.

Snake eagles have large heads covered with long feathers that fan out. They also have short, stubby toes. These toes help them catch and hold on to wriggling snakes.

The long-crested snake eagle perches as high as it can in order to watch for prey.

*The harpy eagle hunts monkeys and sloths.*

Giant forest eagles live in the rain forests of South America, New Guinea, and the Philippines, where they hunt lemurs, monkeys, and sloths. There are only six species. These eagles are among the world's largest and most powerful birds of prey. The harpy eagle of South America is the biggest eagle in the world, and the Philippine eagle is the second biggest. Unfortunately, as rain forests are cut down, many giant forest eagles are in danger of disappearing forever.

14

*The golden eagle has a majestic mantle of feathers on its head and neck.*

Because the legs of *booted eagles* are covered all the way down with feathers, they look as if they are wearing boots. They are not fussy eaters, and so they can live practically anywhere in the world. There are thirty different kinds, and they come in all sizes, from very small to very large. The golden eagle, the largest one, is also the most common. It inhabits treeless areas, such as deserts, grasslands, and the Arctic regions, and mountain ranges, such as the North American Rockies and the Himalayas.

Once eagles around the world enjoyed their hunting and breeding areas with little interruption. Today, a lot of their traditional territory has been lost because of the development of cities, reservoirs, and dams, and the search for minerals and oil. When trees are cut down, shorelines changed, and roads built, eagles must search out new areas in which to live. Fortunately, there are still stretches of deserts, grasslands, rain forests, and high mountains that remain untouched, providing good habitats for eagles.

*The African veldt is the home of snake eagles.*

*Deserts in the American
Southwest are the habitat of
the golden eagle.*

# NATURE IN BALANCE

All eagles are *predators*, animals that survive by hunting, killing, and eating other animals. While this may sound cruel, predators actually help keep the natural world in balance. Predators usually capture weak and sick animals, which are easier to catch. In this way, eagles help healthy animals survive by preventing the spread of disease. Predators also help to keep the population of prey animals under control. This is important because if there are too many animals, there won't be enough food for them all. Some predators, such as eagles, are a great help to farmers as well, because they catch rats, mice, and other animals that destroy crops used for human food.

*The rare white-breasted sea eagle lives in Australia.*

# BIRDS OF PREY:
## COMPARATIVE SIZES

Eagle

Vulture

Falcon

Hawk

# The Perfect Hunter

To be a good hunter, a bird needs far-seeing eyes, powerful feet, a sharp beak and strong jaw muscles, and speed and skill in flying. Eagles have all of these things.

## EAGLE EYES

Anyone who is called "eagle-eyed" has earned high praise. The eagle's eyes are amazing organs. They are set closer to the front of the head than those of many other birds, so that, like humans, the eagle has 3-D, or *binocular*, vision. This helps the eagle to judge distance and speed. For example, if a golden eagle spots a rabbit, not only can the eagle see its prey from more than half a mile away, the eagle's binocular vision helps it to judge how far away the rabbit is and how fast the eagle must fly in order to catch the rabbit.

Some eagles have eyes that are larger than humans' eyes, and their vision may be about eight times sharper. But the eagle sees so well only in the daytime. Unlike the owl, which hunts at night, the eagle doesn't see well in darkness. That is why eagles rest at night and hunt during the day.

Eagles also use their keen eyesight to keep track of other eagles. Each one guards its own hunting ground very carefully, and it may attack another one that tries to hunt in its territory.

*Eagles have keen eyesight. Their eyes are set closer to the front of the head than those of other birds, giving them 3-D, or binocular, vision.*

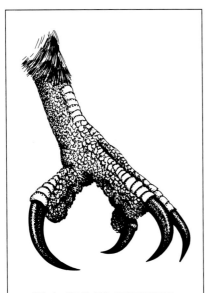

## EAGLE FEET

An eagle's foot has four toes. Three toes point forward and one points backward. Each toe is tipped with a thin, razor-sharp talon. Just before reaching its prey an eagle swings its feet forward. Its feet lock on the prey, and the eagle flies to a perch where it can eat its meal.

# FEARSOME FEET

Eagles use their feet to catch and kill their prey. The foot of an eagle has four toes, and each toe is tipped with a thin, sharp-pointed claw called a *talon*. The toes and talons of each kind of eagle differ slightly because each goes after different prey. If you look at the size of any eagle's foot, you can guess the size of its prey. The eagles that hunt the largest animals have the largest feet and talons.

The harpy eagle of South America is the most powerful eagle in the world. It has thick legs and huge feet and toes that are up to five inches (13 cm) long. The harpy preys on monkeys, which it seizes from treetops and kills with its talons.

Others, such as the golden eagle, one of the booted eagles, have shorter toes and talons because their prey is smaller, but their grip is very strong.

Booted eagles vary in size and diet more than any other group of eagles. Thus, they show the greatest variation and specialization in their feet. Some of the smaller booted eagles of Africa prey on songbirds. These eagles have slim legs and toes which they use to catch their prey in midair.

Of all the eagles, the Indian black eagle has the most unusual feet – long, thin toes and talons that are nearly straight. It snatches up birds' nests that are full of eggs or young birds.

Snake eagles have short, stubby toes that can surround the body of a snake completely. Most snakes are quite fragile and their backbones are easily broken. By simply clutching the snake, the eagle can break the snake's back. Snake eagles also

have thick scales on their legs that protect them from the bites of venomous snakes.

Fish eagles have feet that are good for picking up fish. The undersides of their toes are covered with rough bumps to help them hold on to their slippery catch as they carry it to shore.

*The rough bumps on the toes of a fish eagle help it to hold on to fish.*

*The harpy eagle of the South American rain forests has powerful feet and toes, enabling it to seize monkeys.*

All eagles attack their prey in the same way. Just before it strikes, an eagle opens its wings to slow down and thrusts its legs straight forward so that the feet hit with the full force of its flight behind them. So powerful is this that the blow alone often is enough to kill the prey.

*The golden eagle eats a variety of prey, including rabbits, deer, and sheep.*

# BUTCHER BEAKS

The large, fierce-looking beak of an eagle is well designed to cut, tear, and crush. It is controlled by strong jaw muscles. Just as the feet of eagles differ depending upon what the particular eagle hunts, so do the beaks.

The Philippine eagle has a huge beak to tear apart large prey, such as monkeys or deer. Snake eagles, on the other hand, have smaller beaks because they do not tear their captives apart. Usually they swallow small snakes whole.

## THE CERE

Eagles have an area of bare skin, called the *cere*, at the base of their beak. In some eagles the cere is the same color as the beak; in others it may be a brightly colored blue, red, or yellow. The cere is where you find the eagle's nostrils, through which the bird breathes. Eagles do not have a good sense of smell, so they never use their noses to find their prey.

Cere

An eagle's beak, like its talons, is made of the same kind of material as our fingernails. When an eagle hunts, it wears down its beak and talons, but these grow back continuously, like fingernails. Even when eagles are kept in zoos, their beaks and talons continue to grow. Since the captive birds don't hunt for their food, however, they never wear down their beaks and talons, and these grow longer than normal.

*This golden eagle is using its beak to tear apart a rabbit.*

# EAGLE EARS

Eagle ears are not visible, but like all birds, eagles have them and they hear very well. Their ears are hidden under a layer of special feathers just behind their eyes.

Eagles don't use their ears very much when they are hunting. Mostly they use their ears to listen to one another, or listen for storms, which produce sounds that eagles can hear. This ability is important because the sounds warn the eagles that bad weather is coming. In storms, eagles must land and find shelter, for if an eagle gets soaked in the rain, it may not be able to fly. Also, if the stormy weather lasts for a long time, the eagle may use all its energy trying to stay warm and dry and may not have enough energy left to hunt.

*An eagle's ears are hidden by feathers behind the eyes.*

*This harpy eagle can hear sounds of forthcoming storms.*

# SOARING SKILL

To fly, birds need a light body and wings that are big enough to lift them off the ground. Some birds, like the penguin, don't need to fly. The penguin catches fish in chilly Antarctic waters, so it needs a well-insulated body and flipperlike wings in order to swim.

The eagle, however, is built for flying. It looks much heavier than it really is because of all its feathers. A bald eagle is covered with about seven thousand feathers and weighs approximately eleven pounds. Eagles weigh so little because most of the large bones in their bodies are hollow.

## EAGLE WINGS

If you looked at the bones in an eagle's wing, the bones would look much the same as they do in your own arm.

The primary feathers at the tip of the wing are the most important wing feathers. The eagle can move them like fingers to get a steadier ride in strong winds. The eagle also uses its primary feathers when it takes off and lands.

Sometimes an eagle must travel long distances to find food. If the eagle goes for a whole day, or even several days, without food, it may not have a lot of energy to spare for flapping its wings. Thus eagles have become experts in soaring.

Soaring is a wonderful way to fly without using a lot of energy. Eagles and other soaring birds use *thermals* – warm air currents that rise from the ground and go many miles up. The birds fly into these invisible currents and use them like elevators to lift themselves high into the sky. Sometimes a strong wind will push a thermal along, and the eagle will stay with the thermal to get where it wants to go. When there is no wind, the eagle can circle in the thermal, rising higher and higher, then glide out across the sky for several miles, all the while losing altitude, until it reaches another thermal in which it can rise again.

*A Bateleur eagle displays its plumage.*

*Gliding over its territory, a bald eagle displays its magnificent wingspan. Eagles often use warm air currents, or thermals, to lift themselves high into the sky.*

Another way for the eagle to get a free ride is to find a place where the wind hits a mountain or a wall of trees and can only go up. The heights an eagle can reach by riding on air currents give the bird a panoramic view of the landscape so that it can spot any prey.

# HOW EAGLES USE AIR CURRENTS

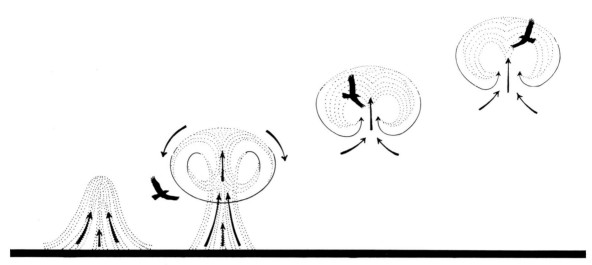

Warm air rises to form a
thermal. An eagle flies into
a thermal and uses the air
current to rise and soar
effortlessly.

Winds blowing against a
hillside form strong
upcurrents which an eagle
uses to get a free ride.

# HOW EAGLES HUNT

Depending on the kind of food they are after, eagles hunt in several different ways. An eagle may sit patiently on a high branch or cliff, where it has a clear view of its surroundings. Or the eagle may soar around or hover in midair until it sees a creature it wants.

Once it has spotted the prey, it folds its wings and swoops down like a dive-bomber. At the last minute, just before contact, it opens its wings to slow down, swings its powerful legs forward, and snatches the prize in its talons.

Sometimes an eagle will make a sneak attack on a possible meal instead of dive-bombing it. A golden eagle, for example, may stalk a rabbit this way: From high above, the eagle sees the rabbit sitting in the shade beside a bush. The eagle flies down far from the rabbit and flies low on the other side of the bush, using the bush to hide its approach. Then – *whoosh!* – the eagle zooms over the bush and grabs the rabbit.

A fish eagle often uses a sneak attack to catch water birds. The eagle flies over the water, using the troughs between waves as its cover. At the last moment, it flies over the wave and snatches the bird out of the water. Sometimes it soars above the water until it spots a fish. Then it swoops down and snatches it in its talons. It then flies to land to eat its catch.

*A bald eagle prepares to eat
a fish that it has just caught.*

Eagles can also be pirates – that is, they sometimes steal food from other birds. Fish eagles, for instance, will steal from pelicans, storks, herons, and ospreys, which are also fish-eating birds. The eagle will chase the other bird until it drops the fish. Then the eagle will catch the fish before it reaches the ground or the water. A fish eagle will steal food not only from other birds but also from other eagles – from its relatives, its young, its mate. The African fish eagle will even steal from other eagles when it isn't hungry, just to show who is boss!

Snake eagles regularly steal snakes from one another, and many booted eagles steal whenever they can. The tawny eagle of Africa is such a fierce pirate that it steals from eagles much bigger than itself.

## EAGLES FISHING

**A fish eagle snatches fish out of the water and flies to land, clutching the prey in its talons.**

*The bold tawny eagle steals from eagles much bigger than itself.*

Eagles usually hunt and kill their own food, but they will also eat mammals, birds, and fish that are already dead. Every year in the late fall, thousands of bald eagles gather on the banks of the Chilkat River in Alaska. There they feast on the salmon that have died after spawning (laying their eggs). As many as three thousand eagles have been seen there.

When dead whales or seals wash up on shore, several bald eagles may feed on them together, returning day after day to stuff themselves until they can barely fly.

The golden eagle, unlike the bald, usually eats alone. It will eat the remains of a deer or moose that was killed by other predators, or it may feed on the carcass of an elk that was too weak to survive. The tawny eagle in Africa will go after dead animals that have been killed by poachers or by lions.

*A tawny eagle feeds on a jackal. It will also eat carrion left by other predators or animals killed by poachers.*

Around the world, many animals are killed by cars as they attempt to cross roads and highways, and eagles often feed on these dead animals. Or they will scavenge at garbage dumps, perching in tall trees around the dump and swooping down to pick through the refuse.

*This golden eagle is spreading its wings over its prey to prevent other eagles from snatching its catch.*

# What Eagles Eat

Eagles eat just about anything – insects, fish, reptiles, other birds, mammals. Each eagle group tends to specialize in certain foods, but since the food they like the most may not always be available, they also eat other things.

## FISH EAGLES

When lakes and rivers start to freeze and fish eagles can no longer hunt fish, they go after ducks and other water birds that have not yet migrated. The eagles often chase sick and injured birds, but they will also hunt healthy ones. Sometimes the eagles work in pairs to catch ducks. First one eagle attacks the duck and forces it to dive underwater. Then when the duck comes up for air, the other eagle will attack it. This keeps up, with the eagles taking turns in attacking, until the duck is too tired to escape anymore.

In some lakes in Africa where there are no fish, the African fish eagle will hunt flamingos and young spoonbills and herons. Fish eagles that live near tropical ocean waters will hunt sea snakes that come to the surface of the water to breathe.

Although the vulturine eagle of Africa is called a fish eagle, curiously enough, it never eats fish! It eats fruit, especially the fruit of palm trees. It is the only eagle in the world that is a vegetarian.

The bald eagle is a fish eagle.

Salmon is an important
source of food for fish eagles.

# SNAKE EAGLES

Snake eagles eat snakes of all sizes and kinds, even poisonous ones. A small poisonous snake dangling from an eagle's talons is probably not powerful enough to twist, rear up, and strike the eagle. The bird kills the snake by gripping it close to the head and eventually crushing the head with its talons or beak. If the snake is not too big, the eagle swallows it head first while flying. Swallowing the snake and its venom does not harm the eagle.

Snake eagles also attack large snakes such as puff adders, killing them by dropping on them and squeezing them tightly with their short, strong toes

## EAGLE PREY

**Eagles eat a variety of prey, from snakes, rabbits, frogs, and fish, to birds, monkeys and mountain sheep.**

and talons. However, they do not swallow these larger snakes in midair. Instead, carrying them with their feet, the eagles fly back to their nests where they swallow the snakes whole. Sometimes the snake may try to strike back, but the snake eagle has thick feathers and layered scales on its legs to help protect it.

The brown harrier eagle of Africa, typical of many snake eagles, has armored legs and a thick pad of feathers on its breast to protect it from a snake that tries to bite it.

Very large snakes such as mambas and cobras are too heavy and dangerous to carry, so they are usually killed on the ground and eaten on the spot. Sometimes the snake eagle brings leftovers back to its nest or perch.

Smaller snake eagles add lizards and frogs to their diet, and larger ones also eat birds.

*Snake eagles kill and eat all kinds of snakes, even rattlesnakes.*

43

# GIANT FOREST EAGLES

These eagles usually hunt animals that live in trees, such as monkeys and sloths. A sloth can hold on to a branch with a very tight grip, but the harpy eagle, with its strong feet, can pull the sloth right out of the tree.

Some giant forest eagles perch in trees along riverbanks, hunting opossums, birds, snakes, and lizards, as well as monkeys. The Philippine eagle glides over the treetops looking for monkeys and large birds such as hornbills.

*Booted eagles prey on many small animals, including the hoary marmot.*

# BOOTED EAGLES

The most numerous and common of eagles, these birds live in many different regions. Thus they have the most varied diet of any of the eagle groups.

The golden eagle, which is one of the largest booted eagles, most often hunts medium-sized animals, such as jack rabbits, but it will go after anything from frogs, lizards, and birds to young deer, sheep, and goats.

In Africa, booted eagles frequently prey on young gazelles and on the tiny dik-dik, one of the smallest gazelles in the world. An adult dik-dik looks like a miniature deer no taller than your knees!

One of the most surprising foods that booted eagles in Africa eat is termites. During the rainy season, termites fly out of their nests in great numbers. From a distance, the swarming termites look like clouds of smoke. Tawny eagles stand by the nests and pluck termites out of the air and from the ground.

Except for snake eagles, which often eat their prey whole, eagles tear their food apart. When they catch a bird or a mammal, they first pluck the feathers or the fur and remove indigestible parts like the stomach, the skull, and the larger bones. Eagles can digest most of what they eat, including small bones, but when they swallow things they cannot digest, such as feathers, fur, birds' beaks, and the scales from fish or snakes, they sometimes regurgitate them in the form of a pellet.

*Monkeys are often the prey of giant forest eagles.*

# Eagle Families

Most eagles are old enough to have a family, or *breed*, when they are four or five years old. By that time they are able to hunt well enough to provide food for their young.

When they are ready to breed, the eagles find mates. Scientists believe that an eagle stays with the same mate for life. If one of the eagles dies, however, the other eagle will look for another mate.

No one knows for sure how long eagles live in the wild, but one North American golden eagle was believed to have lived for more than twenty years. Bald eagles may have a similar life span.

*Scientists believe that eagles stay with the same mate for life.*

SKY DANCING

Approach      Dance      Release

# COURTSHIP

Once a male and female eagle have selected each other as mates, they soar through the sky together, making big loops, rolling over, and plunging in steep dives.

The most spectacular sky dancers are the fish eagles. The dance begins when both birds are high in the sky. The male flies above the female and then swoops down on her with his feet and talons outstretched. As he approaches, the female rolls over on her back and reaches out with her feet. The two grab each other's feet and, with their talons locked together and their wings spread wide, tumble toward the earth with incredible speed. Just when you think they are going to crash, they break apart, fly upward, and begin all over again.

Eagles sky-dance during the early period of courtship, until they are ready to start building their nests.

# BUILDING A NEST

Most eagles build their nests in the early spring. It takes many weeks of hard work to build a nest, and the eagle couple usually build it together.

The nest is made of branches and sticks that the birds pick up from the ground with their feet or beaks. Sometimes if an eagle spots a branch on a tree that is just the right size, it flies toward the branch at full speed and hits it with its feet. The branch breaks off and the eagle carries it away.

Often the male eagle is the collector and the female the architect-builder. Sometimes the female collects the material, too, and sometimes she builds the nest all by herself.

Once a pair of eagles have built a nest, they will probably use the same one year after year. Every spring they will repair the nest by adding more branches to it, so it gets larger each year. One bald eagle's nest in Florida was twenty feet high – higher than a human house! In general, fish eagles build the largest nests and snake eagles the smallest.

Eagles prefer to nest in high places and will build at the tops of tall trees or high on rocky cliffs, if there are no trees. When there is no other choice, they will build their nests on the ground.

The nest is now the eagles' home, and the area around it is called the *nesting territory*. No other eagles are allowed to nest, hunt, or even sit in this area. If a stranger enters the territory, one of the eagles chases it out. The chase seldom ends in a fight, however, since both birds risk getting hurt if they fight.

*Eagles use the same nest and add new branches to it every year, making it larger.*

# EAGLE EGGS

Most eagle mothers lay two eggs, sometimes three or four; a snake eagle lays only one egg. Eagle eggs are about the size of chickens' eggs. Sometimes they are completely white, and sometimes they have brown spots.

In order for the baby eagles to grow inside, the eggs must by kept warm, or *incubated*. For about a month, the parents take turns sitting on the eggs to keep them warm. When one parent gets tired of incubating the eggs, it calls its mate and they trade places. Each time they do, the new eagle gently turns the eggs so that they are kept warm on all sides. The parent has to be careful not to break the eggs, so it curls its toes as it steps into the nest.

The first egg the mother bird lays is the first to hatch. When the baby eagle is ready to hatch, you can hear it chirping inside the egg! The eaglet must break its shell by itself; the mother and father eagle never help. The eaglet uses a hard little tooth on the tip of its beak to crack the eggshell. This special "egg tooth" drops off after a few weeks.

It takes almost two days of hard work for an eaglet to hatch. When it finally tumbles out of the shell, it is tired and weak and wet from the liquid inside the shell. So it takes its first nap, during which the feathers dry out and the soggy little bird is transformed into a fluffy ball of white down.

When there are two or more eggs, the next one hatches two days later. By the time the second eaglet arrives, the first one is already quite a bit bigger and stronger. The parents always feed the largest eaglet first, so sometimes when there isn't enough food the second eaglet goes hungry and

may starve to death. This is nature's method of balancing out the amount of food available and the number of eaglets to be raised. When the food is scarce, only one eaglet will survive; when there is lots of food, three or even four may be raised.

*Although most eagles lay two eggs, sometimes they lay three or four.*

# GROWING UP

The new eagle parents keep very busy taking care of their young. During the first two weeks after hatching, the eaglets are almost never left alone. One parent, usually the mother, stays in the nest day and night, covering the eaglets with her wings to keep them warm, or to protect them from the hot sun or the rain.

Meanwhile the father hunts and brings food to the nest. Since the eaglets are too small to feed themselves, the mother tears the food into small pieces with her beak and dangles the pieces in front of the eaglets' mouths.

Eaglets are fed two or three times a day, but sometimes it seems that they just can't get enough and they scream continually for more food.

Soon the young wobble to their feet, using their wings like crutches. As they become steadier, they flap their wings and climb about the nest. The large nest is a great place for them to exercise, and they often jump up and down as if the nest were a trampoline.

The eaglets stretch and flap their wings regularly. If a wind is blowing, they may manage to rise in the air above the nest, only to come down with a thump. They pretend to hunt, jumping up and landing with their talons spread, as if they were attacking an animal. Or they grab at sticks in the nest and crush them with their beaks. All this play helps the eaglets develop their hunting skills.

Soon dark feathers begin to replace the fluffy down and the eaglets lose their baby appearance. Now they spend a lot of time combing their new feathers with their beaks, so that the feathers remain fluffy and warm.

At the tops of their tails, most birds have a

*Of these two eaglets, the bigger will always be fed first.*

gland that produces oil. The eagle rubs its beak over the gland to cover it with the oil, which it then spreads over its feathers to make them waterproof. The eaglets learn to do this when they are very young.

*This young bald eagle, nesting in a cottonwood tree in Alaska, will soon be ready to venture out on its own.*

As the eaglets grow, they become bolder. As soon as the mother or father bird arrives at the nest with food, an eaglet grabs the food and pulls it away. The first eaglet to get the food keeps it. If there is more than one eaglet, they will steal food from each other.

At two to three months old, the eaglets' beaks and talons are big and strong, and they can tear prey apart by themselves. Now the parents bring live prey to the eaglets so that they can practice hunting and killing it. One biologist saw a parent eagle bring a large, lively fish to the nest. The fish flopped around while the two eaglets stared at it in surprise. Suddenly, before the eaglets could pounce, the fish flipped right out of the nest!

*A parent bald eagle watches over the nest.*

# FIRST FLIGHT

*A young bald eagle shows a new coat of feathers.*

The average eaglet is ready to leave the nest when it is three to four months old. Some are quite daring. They hop out of the nest, flap their wings, and glide to a nearby tree. Sometimes, however, they are unlucky and miss their target or are unable to slow down enough to land. Then they may crash to the ground or end up in the water. Fortunately, when a young eagle lands in the water it can swim back to shore by using its wings.

For a short while after the eaglet makes its first flight, it usually stays near the nest, because its flight feathers are not fully grown. Gradually, however, the young eagle wanders farther away.

As soon as they become better flyers, the young join their parents in hunting. It takes time for them to become good at it, but eventually the young eagles can hunt on their own.

By the time a young eagle is four or five months old, it is completely independent. During its first months on its own, the young bird often finds food through scavenging or stealing from other eagles. The summer is a very risky time for young eagles and many of them do not survive. Eagles newly on their own move out of their parents' territory and search for an area that is not occupied by other adult eagles. In this way, the young eagles do not have to compete with birds that are older and more skilled at hunting.

*This young eagle has left its parents and is now independent.*

# Traveling Eagles

It is very difficult for eagles to find food when lakes and rivers are frozen and a thick blanket of snow covers the land, so most of the eagles that live in the north travel south to a warmer climate for the winter. Every fall, when the cold weather arrives and the days shorten, their urge to *migrate* is triggered. Eagles of northern Europe fly to southern Europe and Africa, the eagles of northern Asia go to India or Southeast Asia, and the eagles of North America also travel south.

When the eagles travel south, they often stop and gather in large numbers in areas where food is plentiful. The Chilkat River in Alaska is one of these places, because its water doesn't freeze very quickly. North American bald eagles also like to congregate along the east and west coasts, as well as by the Mississippi River, where there are plenty of ducks and fish to eat. The gathering places of bald eagles have become very popular, and tourists from all over the world go to these places each year to watch and photograph the eagles.

After the winter is over, the northern eagles return to their northern homes. Usually they go back to the same nesting area they used before, and partners begin to raise new families. How do they know where to go? Birds find their way by recognizing landmarks and using the positions of the sun and stars to guide them. Some scientists think that the earth's magnetic field may also affect the direction in which birds migrate. They have sometimes put bands on their legs to see where they fly.

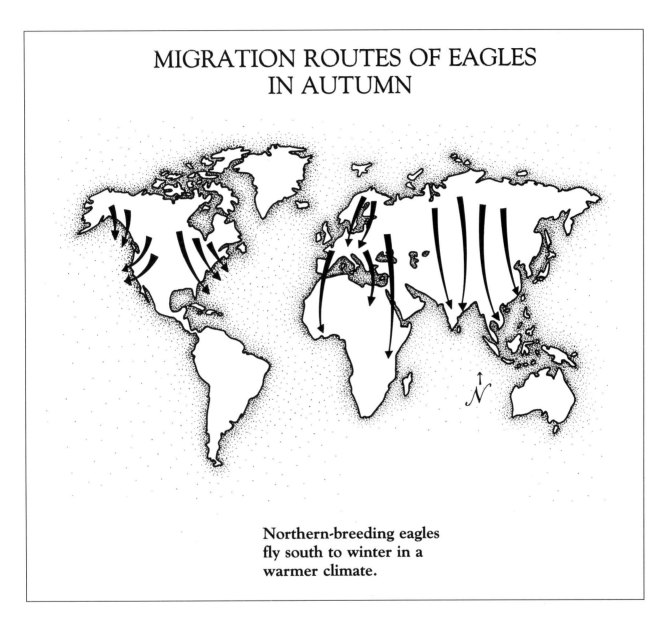

# MIGRATION ROUTES OF EAGLES
# IN AUTUMN

**Northern-breeding eagles
fly south to winter in a
warmer climate.**

The traveling, or migration, of all birds is still
not completely understood. There is a lot to learn
about it. When you think about the enormous
distances they travel and the dangers they face
along the way, you come to appreciate their
intelligence and skill.

# The Future of Eagles

You may think that the eagle has no enemies. Sadly, it does – and its greatest enemy is human beings. Throughout the world, we have destroyed many of the eagles' homes. We have cut down trees where they used to nest, and we have built many highways, cities, and resorts where they used to hunt. We have polluted rivers and lakes with chemicals that kill the fish eagles eat.

In many parts of the world, ranchers and fishermen shoot or poison eagles because they say that eagles catch all their fish and kill many of their livestock. Over and over again this has been shown to be untrue. In the grand scheme of nature, eagles take very little – only enough to survive.

It is against the law, in many countries, to harm an eagle, but people continue to shoot them. Some do, just because the eagle is big and makes an easy target. Some people shoot them to make money. People can sell eagles' bones, feathers, and feet. The feathers alone can be sold for fifty dollars each!

The Philippine eagle is the rarest one in the world. There are only a few hundred of these magnificent birds left in the wild, and they will certainly disappear if people continue to hunt them recklessly and destroy the forests where they live. In the Philippine island of Mindanao, a sanctuary has been set up to protect the eagle, and local people who help preserve the birds receive a reward. In North America, golden eagles and bald eagles are both protected species.

# HOW PESTICIDES MOVE
# THROUGH THE FOOD CHAIN

5. Eagles eat poisoned fish

4. Big fish eat little fish

3. Little fish eat plankton

2. Plankton absorb
   pollution

1. Humans pollute water

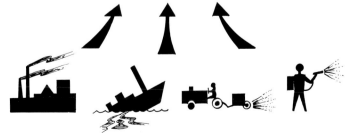

Fortunately, there is still hope for eagles because many people care about them and are committed to their survival. Conservation groups around the world are fighting to protect the areas where eagles live, and to pass laws that will control pollution and stop the shooting and trapping of eagles.

We all have important parts to play in the conservation of these noble birds. Eagles need our friendship and our help in order to survive.

*There are only a few hundred Philippine eagles left in the world.*

# INDEX

Numbers in italics refer to photographs.